MW00364939

What Is the
Gos•pel?

Study Guide

What Is the
Gos•pel?

Study Guide

Greg Gilbert

with Alex Duke

WHEATON, ILLINOIS

Contents

Preface

When I was in elementary school, one of my favorite playground digs was about spelling: "Don't say words you can't spell!" For unathletic kids like me, this was the best we could do.

Years later, I no longer hurl this command at belittling bullies, but I remain a fan of its ethos. We should know how to spell the words we say. But, for the purposes of this book, I want to update the saying a bit: "Don't say words you can't define."

In our era of rejuvenated gospel-centrality, it might sound surprising to you that "gospel" is precisely one of those words. We say it a lot, but I wonder if we can define it. We hear it a lot, but if next Sunday you asked ten church members to tell you what it *means*, I wonder if you wouldn't get ten different answers.

For nearly a decade now, Greg Gilbert's *What Is the Gospel?* has helped Christians and non-Christians alike with this problem. He has helped us to look to God's Word for our definition of this all-important word: *gospel*.

We've written this accompanying study guide for one simple reason: to guide you through that book. The structure is not complicated; the goals are not lofty. It simply walks chapter by chapter through the book, forcing you as the reader to slow down and consider what you've read. These questions are less about content and more about contemplation; less about right answers and more about honest reflection.

Who's it for? I suppose any Christian will profit both from Greg's book and dwelling on the truths of the gospel. But, more pointedly, this study guide is probably best suited for non-Christians or new Christians. Non-Christians will be pushed to consider their standing before the God who made them; they'll be asked to consider what they place their ultimate trust in, and why no answer except the gospel can suffice. New Christians will be instructed in the elementals of their faith; by dwelling on the gospel, they'll lay kindling on their growing affections for Christ.

How do you use it? Alone? One-on-one? In small groups? It doesn't matter. Hopefully, older church members will use this to disciple younger church members, and Christians will use it to evangelize non-Christians. Beyond that, who knows? The Lord is honored as his people sow the seed of the gospel.

There's that word again—*gospel*. Do you know what it means? I hope so. That's an important question. But there's a still more crucial question to consider: Do you believe it?

May God grant many eyes to see, ears to hear, and hearts softened to believe.

Alex Duke
September 2019

Introduction

What Is the Gospel? Summary

There are a lot of definitions of "the gospel." Because some definitions are better than others, we must be discerning. A clear and biblical understanding of the gospel will cause Christians to swell with praise and joy, to grow in confidence as they talk about their faith, and to make sure their churches defend and uphold biblical truth. Similarly, understanding the gospel rightly will provoke non-Christians to think and respond in an informed manner.

Key Texts
Ephesians 3:7–12

1. In your own words, what is the good news of Christianity?

2. On pages 18–20, the author lists several explanations of "the gospel." Do you recognize any of them? Which descriptions seem clear to you, and which seem unclear?

3. How would preserving the edges of the gospel affect our daily lives, our witness, and our confidence? Why is this clarity vital? (See pages 21–22.)

4. Are there ways in which you're tempted to dull the edges of the gospel in conversations with others? Explain.

5. If you're not a Christian, what do you think about what the author says at the end of the introduction: "If there's anything in the world you can't afford to ignore, it is the voice of God saying, 'Good news! Here is how you can be saved from my judgment!'" (p. 22)?

1

Finding the Gospel in the Bible

What Is the Gospel? Summary

We find a reliable summary of Christianity's good news not through Christian tradition or through our experiences and well-reasoned arguments. Instead, we find it through the revealed Word of God, which tells us four things about ourselves:

1. God rules over us as Creator and King.
2. We have sinned against him and are therefore guilty.
3. The solution is not found through our effort but through Christ's sacrifice.
4. We must respond in faith.

Key Texts
Psalm 18:30
Acts 2:14–41
Romans 1:16; 3:10–31
1 Corinthians 15:1–5
2 Timothy 3:16–17

1. In seeking to define the gospel, where do you turn for answers? Why is the Bible the reliable source for defining the gospel truthfully over tradition, human reason, or human experience? (See pages 25–26.)

2. Pick one verse or Bible story that in your mind most clearly depicts the gospel, the message of Christianity. Why did you pick it?

3. Because God is Creator, all creation is accountable to him; all creation (humans included) owe him honor and praise. Have there been times or ways that you've ignored God's rightful authority over your life and not honored or praised him as is his due? Explain. (See page 28.)

4. We need the good news of the gospel because there's also bad news about life in this world. Read Romans 3:10–20 again. What is this bad news—and have you seen this problem play out in your life or the lives of others? (See page 29.)

5. Look at Romans 3:21. Why is Paul's contrast—"But now . . ."—so important and so surprising? What has Christ done to remedy this seemingly unredeemable situation? (See pages 30–31.)

6. Now look at Romans 3:21–31. Paul repeats the word "faith" *eight times* in these eleven verses. Why is this important? (See pages 30–31.)

7. The author summarizes the gospel in four words: "God. Man. Christ. Response" (p. 32). Using these four words, could you explain the gospel in less than 60 seconds? (See page 31.)

2

God the Righteous Creator

What Is the Gospel? Summary

God is the Creator of everything. But the Bible tells us more: he's a righteous and holy Creator who will not overlook sin. Though this might sound like bad news for sinful humanity— and on one level, it is—God's commitment to dealing with sin is good news too, because it proves his trustworthiness and demonstrates his holiness.

Key Texts
Genesis 1
Exodus 34:6–7
Psalm 19
Habakkuk 1:13

1. What adjectives come to your mind when you think about God? (See page 38.)

2. What are a few meaningful implications of God being the Creator of everything? (See page 41.)

3. The author writes, ". . . the fundamental truth of human existence, the well from which all else flows, is that God created us, and therefore God owns us" (p. 42). Is the author overstating the matter? Why or why not?

4. Exodus 34:6–7 teaches clearly that God does not leave the guilty unpunished. Does this reality fit your conception of a God who is also described as loving and merciful? (See page 43.)

5. God is holy and righteous. He's also loving and merciful. These attributes aren't in conflict. But how can this be? What is God's response to sin? (See pages 44–45.) What is his relationship to sinners?

6. Why is the description of "God as an unscrupulous janitor" (p. 44) so ultimately unfulfilling?

7. If God is determined not to overlook sin (Ex. 34:6–7), this means he will not overlook the sins we've committed. The author calls this "bad news" (p. 45), which we'll get to in the next chapter. But before we do, what do you think of this truth? Upon reflection, how does it make you *feel*?

3

Man the Sinner

What Is the Gospel? Summary

To sin means more than to simply "miss the mark." It means to rebel against God our Creator King and, in doing so, sever our relationship with him. Because God is good and just, he will hold us accountable for this sin. This is very bad news.

Key Texts

Genesis 3
Isaiah 59:2
Romans 3:10, 19, 23; 5:12–21
Ephesians 2:1–5
Revelation 6:16–17

1. What is sin? (See page 48.)

2. What are some consequences of Adam and Eve's sin? (See page 50.)

3. Does it jibe with your experience of others that "human beings are fundamentally sinful and rebellious" (p. 51)? Why or why not? What about in your own mind and heart?

4. Why would an understated doctrine of sin diminish our appreciation for what Jesus Christ accomplished on the cross? (See page 51.)

5. According to non-Christians you know, what is humanity's fundamental problem? According to *the Bible*, what is humanity's fundamental problem? (See page 51.)

6. What's the difference between being "guilty of sins" and being "guilty of *sin*"? (See pages 54–55.)

7. Why would you want to make hell sound palatable when sharing the gospel? In what ways have you tried (or been tempted) to do this?

4

Jesus Christ the Savior

What Is the Gospel? Summary

Thankfully, the bad news of God's judgment against sinners isn't the end of the story. Why? Because of the good news of Jesus Christ's perfect life, sin-atoning death, and victorious resurrection. Jesus is the only one qualified to save us—and he did it.

Key Texts

Genesis 3:15
Isaiah 53:4–5
Mark 10:45
John 1:29
1 Corinthians 15:14, 17
2 Corinthians 5:21
Galatians 3:13–14
Hebrews 4:15
1 Peter 2:24; 3:18

1. How does Genesis 3:15 prove that "the Bible is the story of God's counteroffensive against sin" (p. 61)? (See pages 60–61.)

2. Why is it necessary that Jesus is both fully God and fully man? (See pages 61–62.)

3. In what ways was Jesus an unexpected messiah? (See page 64.)

4. Explain the biblical idea of penal substitution in the chart below as it relates both to the Passover and to Jesus himself. (See pages 65–68.)

Passover	Jesus

5. On the cross, God the Father poured out his wrath against our sin onto his Son. Some have called this "divine child abuse." Why is that accusation simply false? (See pages 68–69.)

6. Why is Jesus' resurrection a necessary conclusion to the good news? (See pages 69–70.)

5

Response—
Faith and Repentance

What Is the Gospel? Summary

What we've covered so far are facts of history, wholly accomplished by God himself. They're true, and they've happened, whether people want to acknowledge this or not. And yet, these facts—these works of God—demand a response from us, namely, heartfelt repentance of sin and belief in the person and work of Jesus.

Key Texts

Mark 1:15

Acts 2:38; 3:19; 20:21; 26:18–20

Galatians 2:16

Ephesians 2:1–5

1 John 2:1

1. If faith isn't just believing in something you can't prove, then what is it? (See pages 73–74.)

2. What exactly are we relying on Jesus for? (See pages 75–76.)

3. As we seek to understand salvation, an important Christian doctrine is union with Christ. It simply means that everything Jesus received by merit, Christians receive by grace. What role do faith and repentance play in the Christian's union with Christ? (See pages 76–77.)

4. Explain the uniqueness of Christianity's insistence that we are saved not simply by faith, but by faith *alone*. (See page 78.)

5. Repentance and faith are connected and interdependent; you can't have one without the other. But if we're saved by faith alone, why is repentance necessary? (See page 79.)

6. Why is it impossible to claim Jesus as Savior yet resist him as Lord? (See page 80.)

7. Repentance doesn't mean Christians will be perfect, never sinning again. So what does a repentant posture toward sin look like? (See page 81.)

8. Christians will bear spiritual fruit. But how do we guard against mistaking that fruit—such as good works—for the root cause of our salvation? How do we maintain our reliance on Christ? (See pages 82–83.)

9. If you're reading this book and you're not a Christian, why haven't you yielded yourself to Jesus and put your trust in him? Do you still think your reasons are good enough? If you're reading this book and you are a Christian, is your profession of faith and repentance just as meaningful to you today as it was the hour you first believed?

6

The Kingdom

What Is the Gospel? Summary

The "kingdom of God" is among the most misunderstood biblical ideas. Here's what Christians need to know about it:

- Jesus inaugurated it as proof of his own kingship.
- It's here, but not yet in full.
- It's only a matter of time before God, and God alone, finishes what he started.
- Our entrance into the kingdom is determined by our response to the King.
- Our entrance into the kingdom is expressed here on earth by our commitment to the church.

Key Texts

Matthew 3:2; 13:41–43
Ephesians 3:10–11
Revelation 12:10

1. When the Bible uses the phrase "kingdom of God," what is it referring to? (See page 87.)

2. Is the kingdom of God past, present, or future? (See pages 88–90.)

3. In what sense is the kingdom of God "here"? (See page 88.)

4. If the Christian's eternal destiny isn't just a "never-ending disembodied worship service" (p. 91), then what is it? (See pages 91–92.)

5. Why is it important to remember that only God can con-summate his kingdom? (See pages 92–93.)

6. Upon what is inclusion into God's kingdom based? (See page 93.)

7. A messianic King, a suffering Servant, and a divine Son of Man—Jews in the Old Testament had hoped for all three to eventually come, but they never dreamed those three identities would be wrapped up into a single man. Where in the New Testament does Jesus appropriate these titles for himself, and why is each important? (See page 95.)

8. How is the kingdom of God clarified in the Christian's relationship to a local church? (See pages 97–98.)

7

Keeping the Cross at the Center

What Is the Gospel? Summary

The gospel doesn't make sense apart from the cross of Christ; no one can access salvation apart from repentance and faith. To many people, this sounds exceedingly foolish and narrow, which is why people regularly try to redefine the gospel by centering it on something other than the death and resurrection of Jesus. But any "gospel" that doesn't tell sinners how to stand right before a holy God is no gospel at all.

Key Texts
1 Corinthians 1:23, 25; 2:2; 15:3
Galatians 6:14

1. After what you've learned in *What Is the Gospel?*, are there any ways you feel pressure in your own mind to redefine the gospel or to accentuate some aspects while belittling others? (See page 102.)

2. Why do some say the biblical gospel is too small? And why is that assessment false? (See page 103.)

3. Why is the "Jesus is Lord" gospel too small? (See pages 104–5.)

4. It's true that "God is redeeming a people and remaking the world" (p. 107). But is this message the same as the gospel?

5. What should we think of our role in God's work of "changing the world" for good? What should our expectations be in this regard? (See pages 107–9.)

6. Why is it good news that the gospel sounds like foolishness to the world? (See page 110.)

7. How does embracing the "foolishness of God" (1 Cor. 1:25) give us confidence in the gospel? (See page 111.)

8

The Power of the Gospel

What Is the Gospel? Summary

This side of heaven, Christians are still in a fight against sin. This is why we forget, or sometimes even ignore, the power and beauty of the gospel. What can we do to recalibrate our hearts and minds so that we don't drift toward spiritual laziness? How can we center our lives around this good news so that it propels our everyday living?

Key Texts
Matthew 28:18–20
Luke 24:46–48
Romans 8:31–32; 10:14
Revelation 7:9–10

1. If you're not a Christian and you've finished this book, how has your view of Christianity been challenged? Are you ready to trust Jesus for your salvation? (See page 116.)

2. If you're a Christian, has this book helped you remember that your security is based on Christ's merit and not your own? Explain. Then consider this. Dwell on it. And then rest and rejoice. (See pages 116–17.)

3. How does the gospel inform and motivate our obligation to love Christ's people? Practically speaking, how does this compare to your current relationship with a local church? (See pages 117–18.)

4. God expects his people to share the gospel with others. How can that become a spiritual discipline for you? (See page 120.)

5. In Revelation 7:9–10, John gives us a picture of the end of the world. We know where all this is headed. In what ways does this convict you? In what ways does it encourage you? (See page 121.)

IX 9Marks

Building Healthy Churches

9Marks exists to equip church leaders with a biblical vision and practical resources for displaying God's glory to the nations through healthy churches.

To that end, we want to see churches characterized by these nine marks of health:

1.   Expositional Preaching
2.   Gospel Doctrine
3.   A Biblical Understanding of Conversion and Evangelism
4.   Biblical Church Membership
5.   Biblical Church Discipline
6.   A Biblical Concern for Discipleship and Growth
7.   Biblical Church Leadership
8.   A Biblical Understanding of the Practice of Prayer
9.   A Biblical Understanding and Practice of Missions

Find all our Crossway titles and other resources at 9Marks.org.

Other 9Marks Books

9Marks Series

Building Healthy Churches

Healthy Church Study Guides

Church Questions

NOTES

NOTES

NOTES